The Kids' Around the World Cookbook

Deri Robins

Illustrated by
Charlotte Stowell

Kingfisher
NEW YORK

CONTENTS

KINGFISHER
Larousse Kingfisher Chambers Inc.
95 Madison Avenue
New York, New York 10016

First American edition 1994
10 9 8 7 6 5 4 3 2 1
Copyright © Larousse plc 1994
Illustrations © Charlotte Stowell 1994
All rights reserved under International
and Pan-American Copyright Conventions

LIBRARY OF CONGRESS CATALOGING-IN-PUBLICATION DATA
Robins, Deri.
    The kids' around the world cookbook / by Deri Robins: illustrated
by Charlotte Stowell. – 1st American ed.
        p.   cm.
    Includes index.
    1. Cookery, International–Juvenile literature. [1. Cookery,
International.] I. Stowell, Charlotte, ill. II. Title.
641.59–dc20   93-42504   CIP AC
ISBN 1-85697-997-0
Printed in Spain

GOOD COOK'S TIPS

We're about to set off on a whistle-stop tour of the world's best recipes! All you need is a kitchen, a friendly adult helper, and the ingredients. Most of them can be found in a supermarket. For some you may need to go to a delicatessen.

Before you start, wash your hands and clean your work surface. It's also a good idea to clear up as you go along when you're cooking.

Make sure there's an adult in the kitchen. Someone should *always* supervise when you're chopping, blending, or frying, or when you're taking things in and out of the oven.

Blenders make quick work of mixing liquids — but make sure the lid is on before pushing the button!

Always use an oven glove when taking food from the oven. Put all hot pots and pans on a trivet or a wooden chopping board.

Finally, mop up any spills immediately, before someone slips on them!

(Note: each recipe is enough for four people)

SCANDINAVIA

Sweden, Norway, Denmark, Finland, and Iceland are all part of Scandinavia. There's a lot of coastline around these countries, so fishing is very important — fresh, smoked, and pickled fish of all kinds are served regularly!

Smørrebrød are little open sandwiches. You can use rye crispbreads, crackers, or ordinary sliced bread.

SMØRREBRØD

Here are some typical Danish toppings:

Shrimp, mayonnaise, and
   hard-boiled eggs
Sliced or grated cheese with
   tomato and anchovies
Pâté topped with crisp bacon
Salami or cold ham with
   pickles
Sardines and cucumber

Or just use your own favorite toppings!

1 Butter several slices of bread. Arrange toppings on top, and decorate with some of the following:

2 Tomatoes — these look good if you cut them in a kind of zigzag, as shown in the picture.

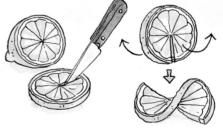

3 Cucumbers — run a fork down the sides before slicing, to make attractive flower shapes.

4 Lemon slices — these look pretty if you cut from the center to the edge, and twist as shown.

It's early in the morning on December 13th — the festival of St. Lucia. All over Sweden, small girls in traditional costume bring spicy gingersnaps to their sleeping families...

GINGERSNAPS

You will need:
1/2 cup butter
5/8 cup brown sugar
1 egg white
1 3/4 cups flour
1/2 tsp. baking soda
1 tsp. ground ginger

Set the oven to 350°F.

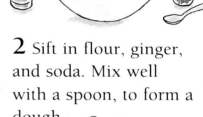

1 Beat the sugar and butter until light and fluffy. Add the egg white, and beat well.

2 Sift in flour, ginger, and soda. Mix well with a spoon, to form a dough.

3 Sprinkle some flour onto your work surface, and roll out the dough carefully until it's about 1/4 inch thick.

4 Use cookie cutters to cut out shapes. Put them on a greased cookie sheet, and bake in the oven for ten minutes.

5 Try decorating the cookies with confectioners' sugar mixed with a little water and food coloring.

NETHERLANDS

The Dutch are famous for their canals, their colorful tulips, their round, fat globes of Edam cheese — and their apple pancakes!

APPLE PANCAKES

You will need:
1 cup flour
Pinch of salt
1 1/3 cups milk
1 large egg
2 tbsp. butter
3 large eating apples
1 tbsp. water
Small bar of chocolate

1 Sift the flour and salt into a bowl. Beat the egg and milk into the flour, to make a batter.

2 Peel, core, and slice the apples. Put them in a pan with the water, and simmer for five minutes.

3 Melt a little butter over a gentle heat in a small frying pan. Pour in enough batter to cover the bottom.

4 Lift the pancake out when it's cooked on both sides. Put it into a warm oven while you make the next one.

5 Put some apple on each pancake, and fold in half. Top with grated chocolate.

GREAT BRITAIN

In Britain, Italian pizzas and Indian curries are now as popular as traditional roast beef and Yorkshire pudding! These three recipes are both delicious *and* traditional....

ENGLISH SUMMER PUDDING

You will need:
$3^1/_3$ *cups mixed berries*
  (raspberries,
  strawberries,
  blackberries, etc.)
$1^5/_8$ *cups sugar*
About 6 slices of slightly
  dry sliced white bread
1 tbsp. water

1 Wash the fruit. Take out any stalks. Put the fruit, sugar, and water in a pan, and cook gently for three minutes.

2 Cut the crusts off the bread. Use all but one slice to line the bottom and sides of a 1 quart mixing bowl.

3 Fill the bowl with the cooked berries, and make a lid from the last slice of bread.

4 Put a flat plate on top of the pudding, and press it all down with a heavy can.

5 Put it in the refrigerator overnight. Turn out onto a plate, and serve with whipped cream.

SCOTTISH OAT COOKIES

If you thought that oats were just for making cereal with, think again....

You will need:
1/4 cup brown sugar
1/4 cup sugar
7/8 cup butter
2 tbsp. corn syrup
5/8 cup flour
1 tsp. baking powder
1 1/3 cups rolled oats
1 egg

Heat oven to 350°F.

1 Beat the butter with the sugars until light and fluffy. Add the egg and syrup, and mix well.

2 Sift in the flour and baking powder, and add the oats. Stir until well mixed together.

3 Put heaped teaspoons of the mixture onto a greased cookie sheet, and flatten slightly.

4 Bake for 12 minutes, then lift onto a cake rack. The cookies will be slightly soft, but they'll become firm and chewy when they cool down.

WELSH RAREBIT
(sometimes called *Welsh Rabbit*)

There's no rabbit in this dish — just cheese, with a dash of milk and mustard!

You will need:
4 slices of bread
3 tbsp. milk
5 oz. cheddar cheese
1 tsp. mustard
Pinch of salt and pepper
Butter or margarine

1 Grate the cheese, and mix with the mustard and milk — this makes the "rarebit."

2 Toast each slice of bread lightly, and then take it out of the broiler or toaster.

3 Butter the toast, and spread with the rarebit. Put under the broiler until brown and bubbly.

GERMANY

There are well over a thousand different types of sausage made in Germany! They were originally made from wild boar (though most are now made from pork), and they are eaten at all times of the day...

To serve these dumplings at their best, leave them to cool down — then cut them into slices and fry in a little butter. They go well with any meat dish.

BAVARIAN DUMPLINGS

You will need:
3 ½ oz. bacon
½ tbsp. oil
6 slightly stale rolls
  (about a day old)
1 ⅛ cups milk
3 eggs
1 tbsp. parsley
Pinch of salt and pepper

1 Chop the bacon. Heat the oil and fry the bacon pieces until golden brown.

2 Cut up the rolls, and put them in a bowl. Heat the milk, and pour it over the bread.

3 Stir in the eggs, parsley, salt, pepper, and bacon. With damp hands, form little balls from the dough.

4 Half-fill a big pan with water, and bring to the boil. Turn off the heat, and drop in the dumplings.

5 Leave for about 20 minutes — when they bob up to the surface, they're ready!

SWITZERLAND

Fondues are for sharing! Put the big dish in the middle of the table, and take turns to dip in bite-sized pieces of crisp vegetables and crusty bread....

SWISS FONDUE

You will need:
1 tbsp. butter
1 clove garlic
1 tsp. cornstarch
$1^1/_3$ cups apple juice
8 oz. Emmenthal cheese (the hole-y kind)
8 oz. cheddar cheese
Salt and pepper
$^1/_2$ tsp. ground nutmeg
Nice things to dip:
chunks of apple, carrot, crusty bread, etc.

1 Crush the garlic, and grate the cheese. Melt the butter, and cook the garlic for one minute.

2 Blend the cornstarch with a little water. Add to the pan, along with the juice and the cheese.

3 Cook over a low heat for five minutes, stirring with a wooden spoon. Add the nutmeg, salt, and pepper.

4 Pour into an oven-proof dish. A food-warmer will keep the pot hot — but an adult *must* help.

FRANCE

French cooks always choose the very finest, freshest ingredients. They often cook them quite simply — as you'll see from the recipes shown here.

SALAD NIÇOISE

You will need:
2 eggs
4 tomatoes
4 green onions
$\frac{1}{2}$ crisp lettuce
1 green pepper
8 oz. can tuna in oil
2 oz. green beans
10-12 canned anchovies
$\frac{1}{2}$ cup black olives

For the dressing:
4 tbsp. olive oil
2 tbsp. wine vinegar
1 clove garlic
Pinch of salt, pepper, and sugar

1 Boil the eggs for ten minutes. Put in cold water until cool. Boil the beans for eight minutes, then drain them.

2 Slice the tomatoes, onions, and pepper. Put them in a bowl with the beans and lettuce.

3 Drain and mash the tuna. Peel and slice the eggs. Arrange the eggs, tuna, anchovies, and olives on the salad.

4 Peel and crush the garlic. Mix with the other ingredients for the dressing. Pour over the salad, and serve at once.

12

CHOCOLATE DELIGHT

You will need:
- 7 oz. milk chocolate
- 1³/₄ pints thick yogurt
- ¹/₂ oz. extra chocolate (for decoration)

1 Break up the chocolate, and put it in a heatproof bowl. Stand the bowl in a pan of boiling water.

2 Stir the chocolate until it melts, then leave it to cool. Fold it into the yogurt.

3 Pour it into serving dishes. Top with extra yogurt, and grate extra chocolate over the top. Chill for one hour.

4 If you prefer, you could flavor the yogurt with orange or lemon juice (add honey or sugar to sweeten).

Snails in garlic butter are a big favorite in France. The French are so fond of these mouthwatering mollusks that some are specially bred on snail farms.....

SPAIN

Paellas are cooked in all parts of Spain, but the ingredients can vary quite a lot from place to place. The usual rule is that whatever is freshest at market in the morning goes into the pot for supper!

PAELLA

You will need:

3 boned and skinned chicken breasts
$1/2$ green pepper
$1/2$ red pepper
1 clove garlic
1 onion
3 tbsp. olive oil
$1 1/2$ cups long-grain rice
$2 1/4$ cups water
16-oz. can tomatoes
1 tsp. turmeric
$3/4$ cup frozen peas
8 cooked shrimp
8 cooked mussels
  (if you like them!)
  Pinch of salt
  Pinch of paprika
  1 lemon

1 Peel garlic and onion. Take the seeds and stalks out of the peppers. Chop them all up. Slice the chicken into thin strips.

2 Heat the oil in a wide, shallow pan, and fry the chicken strips until they turn white. Add the chopped vegetables.

TAPAS are snacks served with drinks in Spanish bars. According to one story they were invented by a barman who used a slice of bread as a lid (a "tapa") to keep flies off his customers' drinks!

3 Add the rice. Cook for a few minutes, stirring all the time.

4 Add the tomatoes, water, turmeric, salt, and paprika. Simmer until the rice is cooked (about 15 minutes).

5 Stir in the peas, and lay the shrimp and the mussels (if used) on top.

6 Cook for five more minutes, then serve with wedges of lemon.

The first paellas were made from snails, eels, and green beans— a slippery and wriggly mixture!

If your paella is too dry it will stick to the pan and start to burn. Add a little more water if necessary— not too much or it will turn into soup!!

ITALY

Italy has it all — beautiful countryside, great art, opera — and some of the most delicious food to be found anywhere on this planet....

PIZZA BASE

To make two bases, you will need:
1 tsp. dried yeast
5 oz. warm water
2¼ cups flour
½ tbsp. olive oil

1 Sift the flour into a big bowl, and add the dried yeast.

2 Add the water and oil. Stir thoroughly until it forms a dough.

3 Knead until smooth and stretchy. Cover with a damp cloth, and leave to rise for 30 minutes.

4 Grease two round, 10-inch pizza pans. Halve the dough, and press each half into a pan.

5 Spread the bases with your chosen toppings, and bake for 25 minutes at 350°F.

One of the fun things about pizzas is that you can mix and match the toppings to your heart's content. Here are a few you might like:

For a basic pizza, spread tomato paste or homemade tomato sauce (see page 29) all over the dough. Top with grated cheese, some dried oregano, and a few slices of tomato.

Spice up the tomato base with some sliced salami, anchovies, onion rings, and a sprinkle of chili powder....

For a breakfast with a difference, try adding some bacon and a fried egg.

Leave out the cheese, and add tuna fish, shrimp (or any other shellfish), olives, and red and green peppers, for a colorful Mediterranean-style pizza.

PIZZA PARTIES

Treat your friends to a pizza party! Make the bases before they arrive, and let them mix and match their own favorite toppings...

QUICK PIZZAS

Lightly toast some slices of bread, then cut into small circles with cookie cutters. Cover with your favorite topping, and put under a medium broiler for a few minutes, until hot and bubbling.

GREECE

Although Greece and Turkey are two very different countries, they both share a lot of the same cooking ideas....

LAMB KEBABS

The lamb in this recipe is soaked in a special sauce called a marinade. (You can skip this stage if you like, but the meat won't be as tender.)

You will need:
4 tbsp. olive oil
1 lemon
Pinch of salt and pepper
1 tsp. dried oregano
1$^{1}/_{2}$ lbs. lean lamb
1 onion
1 red pepper
1 green pepper

1 Squeeze the juice from the lemon. Mix with the oil, oregano, salt, and pepper.

2 Cut the lamb into small cubes. Put it in the marinade, and refrigerate it overnight.

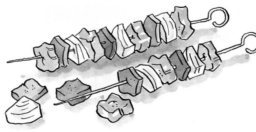

4 Thread the lamb, onion, and pepper onto skewers, as shown above.

5 Broil for 15 minutes, turning now and again until the meat is cooked.

18

It seems likely that the first kebabs were actually cooked by Turkish soldiers who used their swords as skewers!...

TURKEY

3 Peel and chop the onion, and cut the stalk and seeds from the peppers. Chop into small chunks.

Serve the kebabs either on the skewers with a helping of rice, or stuffed into pita pockets, with lettuce and sliced tomatoes....

HUMMUS

This dip uses tahini, a sesame paste, and chickpeas.

You will need:
6-oz. can chickpeas
4 tbsp. tahini
2 lemons
2 garlic cloves
Pinch of salt
2 tbsp. olive oil
Pinch of paprika

1 Peel and chop the garlic, and squeeze the juice from the lemons.

2 Put everything (except the paprika) into a blender, and blend it until smooth. Add a little water if you need to.

3 Pour onto a dish, and sprinkle with the paprika. Serve as a dip with pita pockets.

For a simple, but always wonderful dessert, swirl a tablespoon of honey into a carton of thick yogurt and sprinkle with almonds.

HUNGARY

Although a lot of Hungarian cooking is hot, rich, and warming, this chilled fruit soup is also very popular.

COLD CHERRY SOUP

You will need:
16-oz. can stoneless cherries
  (you could also use
  raspberries or strawberries,
  if you prefer)
⅝ cup water
1 tbsp. cornstarch
⅛ cup sugar
1 tbsp. lemon juice
Small carton sour cream
A few mint leaves

1 Empty the can into a strainer over a pan. Push the cherries through the strainer (mash them in a blender first if this is difficult).

2 Add the water, and cook over a medium heat until the mixture starts to boil.

3 Mix the cornstarch and sugar with a little water. Add this to the soup. Cook for ten minutes, stirring all the time.

4 Add lemon juice. Pour into a bowl, and chill in the refrigerator. Serve with a spoonful of cream and a few mint leaves.

Large areas of Russia are covered by forest — so berries, nuts, and wild mushrooms all play a big part in the cooking.

RUSSIA

Try serving this dish with boiled rice or noodles.

To make homemade smetana, just mix 2oz. plain yogurt with 2oz. of heavy cream.

SMETANA MUSHROOMS

You will need:
1 lb. button mushrooms
3 tbsp. butter
1 onion
1 tbsp. parsley
4 oz. smetana (see above)
A pinch of salt and pepper

1 Wash and dry the mushrooms, and trim the ends off the stalks. Cut them in half, unless they are very small.

2 Melt half the butter in a frying pan. Cook the mushrooms for 15 minutes over a low heat, then spoon into a spare bowl.

3 Chop up the onion and the parsley. Put the rest of the butter in the pan, and fry them gently for ten minutes.

4 Drain the mushrooms, and add to the pan. Stir in the smetana, salt, and pepper, and cook for five more minutes.

More sunflowers are grown in Russia than anywhere else in the world. The seeds are used in salads, or pressed to make oil and margarine.

21

INDIA

Many people in India never eat meat at all. As a result, a lot of the most interesting recipes are vegetarian.

STUFFED PARATHAS

Parathas are a kind of Indian bread. Here, they're stuffed with a mild vegetable curry.

For the stuffing:
2 large potatoes
$1/4$ small head cabbage
8-oz. can sweet corn
1 tbsp. olive or cooking oil
1 onion $1/2$ lemon
$1/2$ tsp. garam masala
1 tsp. ground coriander
$1/2$ tsp. hot chili powder
1 tsp. sugar
Pinch of salt

For the parathas:
$1/2$ tbsp. olive or cooking oil
$1/2$ tbsp. butter
*   large bunch mint leaves*
* $1/2$ tsp. cumin*
* $1/2$ tsp. chili powder*
*   1 tsp. salt*
*   1 tsp. lemon juice*
* $3^1/2$ oz. water*
* $2^1/2$ cups flour*

THE STUFFING

1 Peel the potatoes, and chop into small chunks.

2 Heat the oil, and fry the potatoes gently for a few minutes. Add 2 tbsp. water, and cook until soft.

3 Chop the cabbage, and peel and chop the onion. Add to pan, and cook for another minute.

4 Mash or blend the corn, and squeeze the juice from the lemon. Add these to the pan.

5 Add the spices, salt, and sugar, and mix well. Spoon into a bowl, and leave to cool.

THE PARATHAS

On really special occasions, paper-thin sheets of real gold and silver are used to decorate food, and are eaten as part of the meal....

1 Put the oil and butter in a pan, and heat gently until melted. Pour into a cup and leave to cool.

2 Put the mint, spices, salt, water, and lemon juice into a blender. Blend for a few seconds.

3 Sift the flour, and mix in the oil and mint sauce. Knead it until it makes a stretchy dough.

4 Sprinkle some flour onto your work surface, and divide the dough into eight balls.

5 Make a hole in the top of each ball, and spoon in a little of the curry mixture. Press the edges together.

6 Dust with flour, and roll out the balls until each one is 5 inches wide. Then put a heavy pan over a low heat.

7 Brush each paratha lightly with oil, and fry for a few minutes on each side, until big brown spots appear. Serve with raitha....

BANANA RAITHA

Spoon some plain yogurt into a dish. Peel, trim, and chop two green onions, and add to the yogurt. Peel and slice a banana, and mix this in too.

CHINA

A lot of Chinese food is fried very quickly over a high heat. Our recipe is full of all the right authentic Chinese flavors, but you can just pop it in the oven!

SOY CHICKEN WINGS

You will need:

2 tbsp. soy sauce
1 tsp. Chinese five-spice
1 tbsp. lemon juice
2 green onions
1 tbsp. honey
1 tbsp. tomato paste or ketchup
12 chicken wings
Some aluminum foil

1 Chop the onions. Mix with the soy sauce, spice, lemon juice, honey, and tomato paste in a bowl.

2 Prick the chicken skin, and coat with the sauce. Cover, and leave overnight in the refrigerator.

3 Set the oven to 425°F. Put the coated chicken wings on a cookie sheet lined with a sheet of aluminum foil. Keep the extra sauce!

4 Cook for about 45 minutes, turning them frequently and brushing with extra sauce. They should be crisp, brown, and tender.

Chinese fishermen use specially trained cormorants to help them catch fish!

The Japanese eat rice with all their meals. Most homes have an electric rice cooker, so that there's a supply ready at all hours of the day!

JAPAN

VEGETABLE RICE

You will need:
3 tbsp. cooking oil
2 leeks
1/2 inch root ginger
1 clove garlic
3/4 cup short-grain rice
3 cups water
Pinch of salt
9 oz. green vegetables
(try young spinach,
or frozen peas)

1 Wash, trim, and chop the leeks. Peel and finely chop the ginger. Peel and crush the garlic.

2 Heat the oil in a wok or wide pan. Add the leeks, ginger, and garlic, and fry gently for five minutes.

3 Add the rice, and stir for a few minutes. Add the water and the salt. Simmer for ten minutes.

4 Add the greens to the pan. Simmer for ten minutes, or until the rice is tender.

In Japan, food preparation is a real art. Raw fish and cooked rice are served in neat little packages called SUSHI, while vegetables are carved into all kinds of beautiful shapes.

25

INDONESIA AND THAILAND

The spicy peanut sauce in this recipe is typically Indonesian. (You can also pour it over a bowlful of lightly cooked vegetables — this is called *Gado-Gado*.)

CHICKEN SATAY

You will need:

1 lb. skinless, boneless
  chicken thighs
$^1/_2$ tsp. hot chili powder
$^1/_2$ tsp. sugar
1 tbsp. dark soy sauce
1 tbsp. cooking oil
1 onion
1 clove garlic
2 tbsp. lemon juice
4 tbsp. peanut butter
Pinch of salt
1 tsp. ground cumin
1 tsp. ground coriander
5 tbsp. water

1 Cut the chicken into small chunks. Cook them just like kebabs (page 18) for eight minutes.

2 Mix the chili powder with a little of the water. Peel and chop the onion and garlic, and mix them into the paste.

3 Heat the oil, and cook the onion mixture gently for five minutes. Add the rest of the ingredients, and stir well.

4 Serve the satays with the peanut sauce as a dip.

Coconuts are used a lot in Thai cookery. Monkeys are trained to collect them — they can manage around 500 on a good day!

CORN FRITTERS

In Thailand, street vendors sell little fritters like these from stalls along the street.

You will need:
11-oz. can corn
1 onion
$\frac{1}{2}$ tsp. hot chili powder
2 cloves garlic
1 tsp. ground coriander
4 green onions
3 tbsp. flour
1 tsp. baking powder
Pinch of salt
1 egg
4 tbsp. cooking oil

1 Drain the corn. Crush the kernels for a few seconds in a blender.

2 Peel and chop the garlic and onions. Mix with everything except the oil.

3 Heat the oil, and drop in a few teaspoonfuls of the mixture. Fry gently for three minutes, turn over, and repeat.

4 Drain on paper towels, and serve them while they're hot!

Boats laden with every imaginable type of food come to the floating markets of the Indonesian and Thai waterways...

U.S.A.

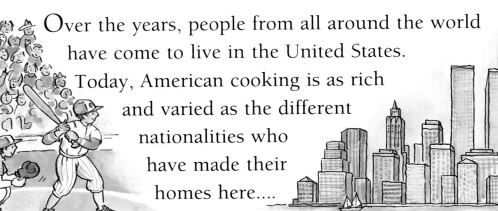

Over the years, people from all around the world have come to live in the United States. Today, American cooking is as rich and varied as the different nationalities who have made their homes here....

The birth of the hot dog (or, how the German sausage became an all-American treat): In 1906, an American cartoonist called Tad Dorgan was idly sketching as he watched a baseball game. He drew some frankfurters and made them look like dachshunds in buns. Underneath he wrote HOT DOGS...

CORNED BEEF HASH

A great favorite for a quick meal.

You will need:
4 medium potatoes
1 big onion
2 tbsp. cooking oil
16-oz. can corned beef
Ketchup

1 Peel and slice the potatoes. Put them in a pan, and cover with water. Bring to the boil, and simmer for 15 minutes.

2 Drain the potatoes, and fry them gently in half the oil until they're brown and slightly crisp all over. Take them out.

3 Peel and chop the onion. Put the rest of the oil in the pan, and cook for ten minutes.

4 Chop the corned beef, and mix with the onions, potatoes, and ketchup. Heat through, and serve.

Fat orange pumpkins are sold in the fall, and pumpkin pie is always a favorite at Thanksgiving dinner.

PUMPKIN PIE

You will need:

A small pumpkin,
*   weighing about 2$\frac{1}{2}$ lbs.*
9 oz. readymade pie
*   pastry*
1$\frac{1}{4}$ cups heavy cream
3 eggs
$\frac{3}{4}$ cup sugar
$\frac{1}{2}$ tsp. salt
1 tsp. ground ginger
1 tsp. ground cinnamon
$\frac{1}{2}$ tsp. ground nutmeg

Set the oven to
400°F for the pastry.

BEST EVER KETCHUP

Chop an onion, and fry gently in 1 tbsp. oil for 5 minutes. Stir in 1 tbsp. cornstarch and cook for 2 minutes. Add a 16-oz. can of tomatoes, 1 tbsp. tomato paste, 1 tbsp. fresh basil, 3 tsp. brown sugar, and a pinch of salt and pepper. Simmer for 5 minutes.

1 Roll the pastry into a circle, and line a 9-inch pie pan. Bake for about 15 minutes, or until golden brown.

2 Scoop the flesh out of the pumpkin, and throw away the skin and seeds. Put in a pan, cover with water, and simmer for 25 minutes.

3 Drain away the water, and leave the pumpkin to cool down. Mash with a fork or in a blender until it's perfectly smooth and free of lumps.

4 Beat pumpkin, eggs, cream, salt, sugar, and spices. Pour into the pie pan, and bake at 375°F for 40 minutes.

Serve the pie with plenty of whipped cream!

HOLLYWOOD
SALAD BOWL

Most of California enjoys warm weather all year round. Salads and health foods are popular here — Californians like to keep themselves fit!

You will need:
1 crisp head lettuce
1 avocado
1 orange
¼ cup pecans or walnuts
3 tbsp. mayonnaise
3 tbsp. plain yogurt
1 tbsp. lemon juice
Pinch of salt and pepper

1 Wash the lettuce leaves, and drain them in a colander or salad spinner.

2 Peel the orange, and chop up the segments. Arrange on the lettuce.

3 Peel the avocado, and take out the seed. Chop into chunks, and sprinkle with lemon juice.

4 Add the avocado and the nuts to the salad.

5 Mix the mayonnaise and yogurt with salt and pepper, and pour over the salad.

SURFER'S SHAKE

Delicious and nutritious!

You will need:
A big glass of milk
1 banana (or other soft fruit)

Throw the ingredients into a blender. Switch on. Switch off. Drink.

CAJUN BREAKFAST SPECIAL

Down in Louisiana, the cooking has a spicy flavor — thanks mainly to the French, Spanish, and Caribbean settlers who have made their home here.

New Orleans is world-famous for its jazz music, wild Marai Gras celebrations, and delicious cooking!

You will need:
6 slices stale bread
2 tbsp. cooking oil
1 onion
1/2 lb. mushrooms
2 cloves garlic
1 stalk celery
4 sausages
6 strips bacon
12 oz. cheddar cheese
4 eggs
2 cups milk
1 tbsp. mustard
1 tsp. cumin
1 tsp. cayenne pepper

1 Broil the sausages and bacon under a medium heat until thoroughly cooked and brown.

2 Peel and chop the onion and the garlic. Wash and slice the celery and mushrooms.

3 Heat the oil in a pan. Cook the vegetables for five minutes over a medium heat.

4 Grate the cheese. Remove crusts and chop the bread into cubes. Chop the sausages and bacon.

5 Put the bread into an ovenproof dish. Top with layers of sausage, bacon, cheese, and fried vegetables.

6 Beat the eggs, milk, and seasonings, and pour over the top. Cover the dish, and leave it overnight in the refrigerator.

7 The next morning, set the oven to 350°F. Take off the lid, and bake the dish for one hour. Serve it hot!

MEXICO

Spicy chilis carry a sting in their tails! Although some Mexicans like to chew the red-hot peppers raw, you'll probably find that a tiny pinch of chili powder goes a very long way....

TORTILLAS

You will need: $1\frac{1}{4}$ cups wholegrain flour; $\frac{1}{4}$ cup margarine or butter; $\frac{5}{8}$ cup warm water; some olive oil

1 Sift the flour into a bowl. Add the margarine, cut up into pea-sized pieces, and stir in the water. Mix into a dough.

2 Divide into 12 balls. Brush with oil, cover, and leave for 20 minutes. On a floured surface, roll into $5\frac{1}{2}$-inch circles.

3 Brush a heavy pan with a tiny amount of oil. Cook the tortillas gently for two minutes on each side, until blisters appear.

4 Put a spoonful of your chosen filling in the middle of the tortilla, fold it over, and serve. Add some grated cheese.

In Mexico there are over a hundred different kinds of chili pepper - some hotter than others!

Did you know that chili peppers, avocados, tomatoes, beans, and TURKEYS all originally came from MEXICO?!!

HOT STUFF!

Try filling your tortillas with some of these sizzling stuffings! Guacamole and salsa also make great dips for tortilla chips....

GUACAMOLE

You will need: 2 ripe avocados; juice of $\frac{1}{2}$ lemon; 1 tomato; 1 green onion; 3 tbsp. sour cream; pinch of salt and chili pepper

1 Chop up the green onion. Peel and chop the tomato. Peel the avocados, cut in half, and take out the seeds.

2 Mix all the ingredients together — either mash them up with a fork, or use an electric blender.

REFRITOS

You will need: 16-oz. can red kidney beans; 1 large onion; 1–2 cloves of garlic; $2\frac{1}{2}$ tbsp. margarine or butter; a pinch of chili pepper

1 Peel and chop the onion and garlic. Melt the margarine in a pan over a medium heat, and fry the onion and garlic gently for five minutes.

2 Mash the beans, and add to the mixture with the pepper. Cook it all through until hot.

SALSA

The Mexican Day of the Dead is celebrated with all kinds of festive food- including little sugar skulls and skeletons!

You will need: 1 small can tomatoes; 1 small onion; hot chili powder to taste (try $\frac{1}{2}$ tsp.); a pinch of sugar; a pinch of salt and pepper

Just peel and chop the onion, and mix it with the rest of the ingredients.

Cool down a hot salsa with a bowl of chilled sour cream and chopped cucumber!

33

CARIBBEAN

Next stop is the Caribbean — a group of tropical islands cradled between North and South America. Get ready for some sunshine cooking!

PINEAPPLE ICE CREAM

You will need:
2 cups milk
$\frac{7}{8}$ cup sugar
3 eggs
$1\frac{3}{4}$ cups heavy cream
Small can crushed pineapple

1 Beat the eggs, and mix them with the milk and sugar.

2 Heat until the mixture starts to thicken. Beat with a whisk, and cool.

3 Whip the cream until it thickens. Fold the cream and crushed pineapple into the custard.

4 Pour the custard into a plastic container. Cover it, and put it in the freezer until firm.

These Caribbean vegetables can be cooked by peeling, chopping into chunks, and boiling in a pan of water until tender. Drain, and add a knob of butter.

ackee

breadfruit

sweet potato

cassava

In the tropical Caribbean climate, bananas grow all year round. They are more than just a food - for example the leaves are sometimes woven together to make roofs.....

BANANA BREAD

You will never want to eat ordinary bread again...

You will need:
2$\frac{1}{2}$ cups flour
1 tbsp. baking powder
1 lb. ripe bananas
$\frac{1}{2}$ cup butter
$\frac{5}{8}$ cup sugar
1 egg
$\frac{1}{2}$ tsp. salt
$\frac{1}{2}$ tsp. grated nutmeg
$\frac{5}{8}$ cup raisins
4 tbsp. chopped pecans

Set the oven to 350°F.

1 Beat the butter and sugar until light and fluffy. Add the egg, and beat thoroughly.

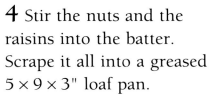

2 Sift the flour, baking powder, salt, and nutmeg into another bowl. Peel and mash the bananas in a third bowl.

3 Beat a little of the flour into the egg. Mix in a little banana. Repeat until flour and banana are used up.

4 Stir the nuts and the raisins into the batter. Scrape it all into a greased 5 × 9 × 3" loaf pan.

5 Bake for one hour. Use a knife to check that the middle is cooked — it should be clean when you pull it out.

AFRICA

Because Africa is a huge continent with over 50 countries, it's hardly surprising that there's no such thing as a "typical" African meal! Here's a slightly spicy dish from southern Africa.

BOBOTIE

You will need:

1 onion
1 tbsp. olive oil
2 slices bread
1 cup milk
1 lb. ground beef
1 tbsp. curry powder
$^1/_4$ cup slivered almonds
$^1/_3$ cup raisins
1 tbsp. lemon juice
Pinch of salt and pepper
2 eggs

Before you start, set the oven to 350°F.

1 Cut the crusts off the bread, break it into chunks, and soak it in half of the milk.

2 Chop the onion. Heat the oil in a pan, and fry the onion over a low heat for ten minutes.

4 Spoon all of it into an ovenproof dish. Beat the eggs with the rest of the milk, and pour over the mixture.

5 Put it in the oven for 1$^1/_4$ hours. The top of the bobotie should be set and golden brown.

Peanuts are grown in many parts of Africa. Try making your own homemade peanut butter. Put 4oz. salted peanuts and 2 tablespoons of vegetable oil into a blender and switch on — the longer you blend, the less crunchy it will be.

3 Add the beef, curry powder, lemon juice, nuts, raisins, salt, and pepper to the pan. Fry until the meat is brown all over.

BAKED BANANAS

African meals usually end with some fresh fruit, or a simply cooked dessert.

You will need:
4 large bananas
2 tbsp. brown sugar
1 tsp. cinnamon
2 tbsp. butter or
*   margarine*

Set the oven to
350°F.

1 Cut the bananas in half lengthwise. Put in an ovenproof dish, with the cut sides facing up.

2 Melt the butter in a pan over a low heat. Stir in the sugar and the cinnamon.

3 Pour over the bananas. Cover the dish with aluminum foil, and bake for 45 minutes.

AUSTRALIA

When the famous ballerina Anna Pavlova toured Australia, a leading chef was so bowled over that he invented this recipe in her honor. The meringues are said to resemble her swirling skirt!

PAVLOVA

You will need:

5 eggs
³/₄ cup sugar
8 oz. heavy cream
12 oz. thick yogurt
1 small can sliced pineapple
2 kiwi fruits
A few sprigs of mint
Waxed paper

Heat the oven to 300°F before you begin.

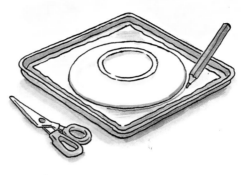

1 Cut a circle from the waxed paper, using a big plate as a guide.

2 Crack the eggs, and separate the whites from the yolks.

3 Whip the whites until they are stiff enough to stand up in peaks — an electric mixer is best for this.

Witchetty grubs are considered to be a great delicacy by some Aborigines. They are said to taste a bit like scrambled eggs.

The Koala bear is a very fussy eater. It will only eat the fresh young leaves from particular sorts of gum tree....

4 Gradually add the sugar, one tablespoon at a time. Whip well before adding each new tablespoonful.

5 Spoon the meringue mixture in a ring on the paper. Bake for five minutes, then lower the heat to 250°F.

6 Bake for 50 minutes, or until crisp on the outside. Leave to cool, then peel off the paper.

7 Whip the cream until slightly stiff, then fold in the yogurt. Pile it in the middle of the ring.

8 Chop the pineapple and kiwi, and arrange on top of the cream. Decorate with sprigs of mint, and serve at once.

SPIDERS!

Fill a tall glass with soda (any flavor you like).

Add a blob of ice cream and a straw.

MIDDLE EAST

Middle Eastern cooking is colorful, rich, and scented with spices. The Middle East is a very hospitable region and food plays a big part in making visitors welcome.

BÖREK

You will need:
8 oz. readymade filo pastry
4 tbsp. olive oil
12 oz. feta cheese
Large bunch of mint
Pinch pepper and nutmeg

Heat the oven to 350°F.

1 Crumble the feta cheese into a mixing bowl. Add the pepper and nutmeg.

2 Wash the mint, and cut up with scissors. Add to the cheese, and mash with a fork until creamy.

3 Take out the pieces of filo pastry and separate carefully. Cut them into strips about 3 inches wide.

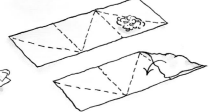

4 Brush strips with oil, and put a teaspoonful of feta in the corner of each one. Fold as here.

A typical Middle Eastern meal begins with a tableful of starters called "mezze." As well as the little pies shown here, you might be offered olives, pickles, nuts, salads, and dips such as hummus (see page 19).

5 Keep folding, so that you end up with fat little triangles. Repeat until all the feta is used up.

6 Brush with oil, and bake on a greased cookie sheet for 25 minutes, or until golden.

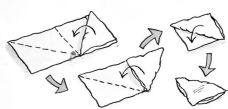